COUNTRIES IN OUR WORLD

SOUTH AFRICA

Ali Brownlie Bojang

W
FRANKLIN WATTS
LONDON·SYDNEY

This edition 2012

First published in 2009 by
Franklin Watts
338 Euston Road
London NW1 3BH

Franklin Watts Australia
Level 17/207 Kent Street
Sydney NSW 2000

Produced for Franklin Watts by
White-Thomson Publishing
+44 (0)845 362 8240
www.wtpub.co.uk

Series consultant: Rob Bowden
Editor: Sonya Newland
Designer: Hayley Cove
Picture researcher: Amy Sparks

A CIP catalogue record for this book is available from
the British Library.

Dewey Classification: 916.8

ISBN: 978 1 4451 0805 6

Printed in Malaysia

Franklin Watts is a division of Hachette Children's
Books, an Hachette UK Company.

www.hachette.co.uk

Picture Credits
Corbis: Cover (Jon Hicks), 5 (David Turnley),
12 (Louise Gubb), 13 (Mike Hutchings/Reuters),
18 (Anthony Bannister/Gallo Images), 20 (Krista
Kennell/ZUMA), 22 (Jonathan Blair), 26 (epa),
27 (Mike Hutchings/Reuters); **Dreamstime:** 1
(Danielvw), 6 (Ankevanwyk), 7 (Ankevanwyk),
8 (Tuckerb34), 9 (Sebcanuto), 11 (Nienie1), 15
(Piccaya), 17 (Danielvw), 21 (Hongqi Zhang), 23
(Felker), 24 (Pg-images); **Fotolia:** 10 (Samuel Birken);
Photoshot: 14 (WpN/UPPA), 19 (Offside/Talking
Sport), 25 (World Pictures); **Shutterstock:** 16 (Victoria
Field), 28 (Michael Jung), 29 (Eye Ubiquitous)

Contents

South Africa is the eighth largest of the 53 countries in Africa. It has the largest economy and has a strong influence over what happens in other African countries. More and more, South Africa is also playing a part in global affairs.

Separated lives

Between 1948 and 1994, South Africa had a system of government known as apartheid, which means 'separateness'. Although about 80 per cent of the population was black, they were not allowed to vote, and white people ran the country. Under this system, black South Africans had to live in separate areas from white South Africans. They had to travel on different buses, go to different schools and even use separate beaches and toilets. All around the world, people campaigned against apartheid.

▼ *The 1994 election was the first in which black people were allowed to vote since the beginning of apartheid in 1948.*

ZIMBABWE

MOZAMBIQUE

BOTSWANA

Limpopo River

Kruger National Park

NAMIBIA

Kalahari Desert

■ Pretoria
○ Johannesburg

SWAZILAND

St Lucia Wetlands

Bloemfontein

Orange River

LESOTHO

Drakensberg Mountains

○ Durban

Atlantic Ocean

SOUTH AFRICA

Fynbos

Indian Ocean

■ Cape Town

Port Elizabeth

N
W — E
S

Key
■ Capital city
○ Other cities

0   miles   300
0   kilometres   300

◀ *South Africa is bordered in the north by Namibia, Botswana, Zimbabwe and Mozambique, and in the east by Swaziland. The independent kingdom of Lesotho lies completely within South Africa's borders.*

An emerging world power

Apartheid ended in 1994, and that year all South Africans – whatever the colour of their skin – were allowed to vote. They elected their first black president, Nelson Mandela. South Africa had been banned from several international organizations and from taking part in some international sporting events because of its apartheid policy. Since 1994, however, it has been welcomed back into organizations such as the United Nations. In 2011 it took on a non-permanent seat on the UN Security Council, the organization that decides what action to take in the event of conflict across the world. South Africa has also improved its relationships with its neighbours in Africa, and has been a major contributor to African Union peacekeeping missions in countries such as Sudan.

Ties around the world

Many South Africans have family ties all over the world, reflecting the many different places from which South Africans – both black and white – originally came. As South Africa has opened up to the world, its links to other countries have strengthened in many ways. South Africa is rich in minerals, and the rapidly developing country of China, which needs lots of resources for its booming industry, has become one of South Africa's main trading partners. South Africa has global links in sporting affairs, too – including playing host to the 2010 football World Cup, attracting sports fans from all over the globe.

IT STARTED HERE

Human ancestors

In 1998, scientists found a complete skeleton in South Africa that dated back more than three million years. It shows that some of the earliest ancestors of humans probably lived in this area.

▼ *Sports stadiums were built and other infrastructures, such as roads, were improved in preparation for the 2010 World Cup finals.*

Challenges ahead

Although South Africa has developed a great deal in the past decade, it still faces many challenges. Just after the end of apartheid, in 1995, South Africa had the highest murder rate in the world. For every 100,000 people, 67 were murdered. By 2011, this rate had dropped to 31.9 murders per 100,000, pushing South Africa down to eighth position in the list of most dangerous countries to live in. Some black South Africans have become wealthier, but for many there are still very few jobs, low wages, poor housing conditions and a lack of good schools. Many black South Africans are still not treated equally with white South Africans. With over 600 deaths a day from HIV/AIDS, South Africa has the highest death rate from the virus in the world.

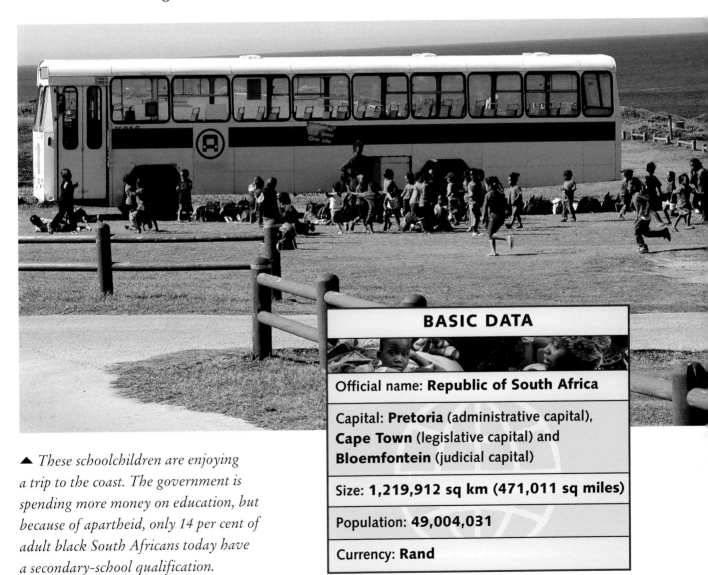

▲ *These schoolchildren are enjoying a trip to the coast. The government is spending more money on education, but because of apartheid, only 14 per cent of adult black South Africans today have a secondary-school qualification.*

BASIC DATA

Official name: Republic of South Africa

Capital: Pretoria (administrative capital), **Cape Town** (legislative capital) and **Bloemfontein** (judicial capital)

Size: 1,219,912 sq km (471,011 sq miles)

Population: 49,004,031

Currency: Rand

Landscapes and environment

South Africa covers the southern tip of the African continent. Its longest border is with the oceans, and it stretches 2,800 km (1,740 miles). Some of the world's most diverse landscapes, animals and plants can be found in South Africa.

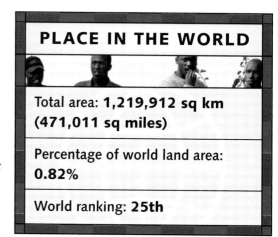

PLACE IN THE WORLD
Total area: **1,219,912 sq km (471,011 sq miles)**
Percentage of world land area: **0.82%**
World ranking: **25th**

The High Veldt

The interior of South Africa is a huge, rolling area of grassland known as the High Veldt. This was once a massive mountain range, but over millions of years it has been worn down into a lower, smoother plateau, with an average height of 1,200 m (3,937 ft). To the north, the plateau meets the southern edge of the Kalahari Desert.

Mountains high

Mountain ranges surround the High Veldt. Along the southern edge they form a series of low ridges that run parallel to the coast. These ridges rise up in the east to form the Drakensberg ('Dragon's Back') Mountains, which contain the highest peak in South Africa – Mount Njesuthi, at 3,408 m (11,181 ft).

▼ *The Drakensberg Mountains stretch around 1,000 km (620 miles) across the east of the country.*

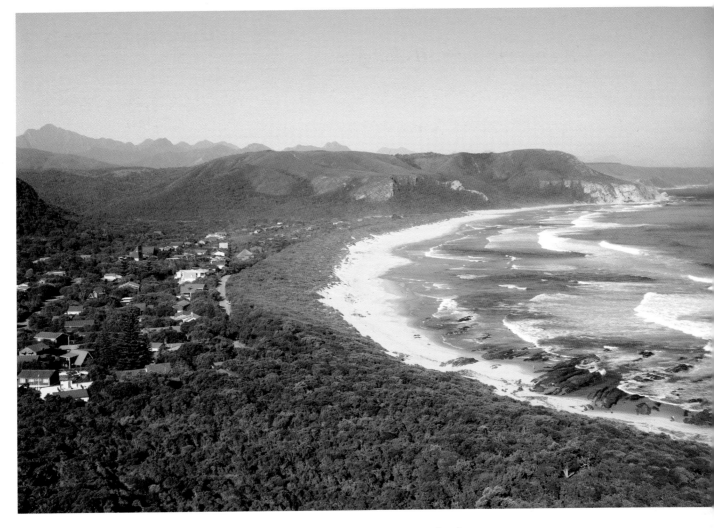

▲ *Nature's Valley, situated on South Africa's Garden Route – a stretch of countryside famous for its pine forests and seaside towns.*

The beautiful south

Between the mountains and the sea lies a coastal plain. The south-west region is one of the most popular tourist destinations for both South Africans and foreign visitors. It has long, sandy beaches and pine forests. This area is also known for producing citrus fruits and wine, which are two of South Africa's main exports.

THE HOME OF...

Table Mountain

Table Mountain, near Cape Town (on cover), is thought to be one of the oldest mountains in the world. It is just over 1,000 m (3,281 ft) high and is six times older than the Himalayas in Asia.

GOING GLOBAL

South Africa has eight UNESCO World Heritage Sites – areas around the world that are considered to be of outstanding natural, historical and cultural value. In South Africa they include Robben Island, where Nelson Mandela was imprisoned, the *fynbos* and the St Lucia Wetlands.

▲ *Robben Island, shown here with Table Mountain in the background, is one of South Africa's eight UNESCO World Heritage Sites.*

Rivers

South Africa has two main rivers. The Orange River is the longest, rising in the Drakensberg Mountains and flowing for 2,200 km (1,367 miles) across the country to the Atlantic Ocean. South Africa's second longest river, the Limpopo, flows eastwards into the Indian Ocean, and forms the border between South Africa and Zimbabwe.

Fauna of the fynbos

The fynbos is a unique area in the Cape region of South Africa. With nearly 8,000 different species, it has the highest concentration of plants in the world, many of which cannot be found anywhere else on the planet. Fynbos means 'fine bush', and the area was given this name because many of the plants are evergreen with fine, needle-like leaves.

Climate

Most of South Africa has a moderate climate, which means it is neither too hot nor too cold. On the High Veldt, summers are warm and winters are cool – sometimes freezing. The east coast has almost a tropical climate, which means it is warm and wet. Summer temperatures are on average around 24°C (75°F), and winter temperatures are around 18°C (64°F). In the east rainfall is high, at around 1,000 mm (39 in) a year. However, this gradually decreases further west, to less than 130 mm (5 in). The west often suffers from droughts, and because this is the main crop-farming region in South Africa, there can be food shortages and people's livelihoods can be threatened.

IT'S A FACT!

The Vredefort Dome in South Africa is the largest meteorite crash site in the world. It was formed two billion years ago. Some scientists believe that the impact could have increased the Earth's oxygen levels, allowing life forms to develop.

▼ *Kruger National Park is one of the world's largest wildlife sanctuaries. Savannah and dense bush make it an ideal home for elephants and many other animals.*

Population and migration

South Africa's population is made up of so many different ethnic groups that it has been nicknamed the 'rainbow nation'. Over thousands of years, people have moved to South Africa from countries all over the world.

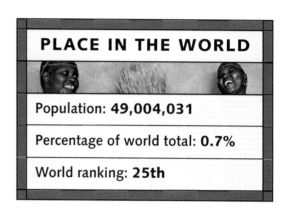

PLACE IN THE WORLD

Population: **49,004,031**

Percentage of world total: **0.7%**

World ranking: **25th**

Who are South Africans?

Black Africans make up nearly 80 per cent of the total population. The rest of the South African population is made up of white people, coloured people (those of mixed race) and people of Asian origin.

▼ *Black and white South African students mix at Cape Town university.*

Where do they live?

Nearly 21 per cent of South Africans live in KwaZulu-Natal province. Gauteng province, containing the largest city, Johannesburg, and the administrative capital, Pretoria, is the smallest but most densely populated province. Although the Northern Cape covers nearly 30 per cent of the country's land area, only 2.3 per cent of the population lives there.

▲ *An HIV-positive patient is shown how to schedule the drugs she must take. This clinic in Cape Town is run by the international organization Doctors Without Borders.*

Growing population

The HIV/AIDS virus seriously affects the growth and life expectancy of South Africa's population. Although the population is growing, the rate of growth has slowed down considerably in the past 20 years. In the 1980s, it grew by 2.4 per cent, but by 2011 this had fallen to 0.38 per cent. The average life expectancy has also fallen, and this is now 49.33 years. It is estimated that without HIV/AIDS, the average life expectancy would be about 15 years more.

IT'S A FACT!

South Africa has the worst AIDS epidemic in the world. In 2009 there were about 5.6 million people living with the HIV virus. An estimated 300,000 of these people were under the age of 15. It is estimated that there are 1.9 million AIDS orphans in South Africa, who have lost at least one parent to the disease.

Moving to South Africa

Over the past 100 years, many people have moved to South Africa. In the 1930s and 1940s, Jewish refugees from Eastern Europe, fleeing from persecution in their own countries, sought refuge in South Africa. Later – throughout the 1970s and 1980s – many people from the UK settled in South Africa, as well as people from China and Portugal. Since the end of apartheid in the 1990s, the majority of immigrants have come from Nigeria as well as parts of Asia, Europe and the USA.

Refugees from Zimbabwe

It is thought that over a million Zimbabwean refugees, fleeing from poverty and conflict in their own country, crossed the border to South Africa in 2008. Some entered illegally and, if they were caught, they were sent back to Zimbabwe. The South African government continues to crack down on Zimbabwean refugees. In 2010 the government brought in a new law to make every Zimbabwean apply for a visa granting them the right to stay, or face deportation. In addition, South Africa has placed military units along the border.

▼ *In 2008, violence increased against immigrants, and many left the country. These people are waiting to board buses to Mozambique.*

City living

During apartheid, black people were forced to live in rural areas, known as 'homelands'. Men left their families to find work in the cities – even though this was often illegal – and lived in settlements set aside for them known as townships. This flow of people to South Africa's cities has continued, but today it is not illegal and people can move wherever they like. Black people are moving into areas of cities where once only white people lived. Today, nearly 60 per cent of South Africans live in cities, and urban areas are growing rapidly.

GOING GLOBAL

Many young, skilled people, such as IT professionals, doctors, dentists, scientists, nurses and teachers, have left South Africa. They go looking for better-paid jobs in other countries such as the UK, the USA and Canada, as well as other African countries. South Africa needs to find a way to persuade skilled people to stay, as they have an important contribution to make to their country's future.

▼ *As more and more people move to the cities for work, townships like this are spreading further out, expanding urban areas.*

Culture and lifestyles

South Africa's music, dance, literature, art and drama have all been influenced by a mixture of African, European and Asian cultures. Like many other countries, modern popular culture in South Africa is also strongly influenced by the USA and Europe.

Traditional art

Some of the earliest art in the world can be found in South Africa. During the Stone Age – up to 35,000 years ago – the Kohl and San bush people lived in the Drakensberg Mountains. They made cave paintings showing what their daily lives were like, often depicting hunting and battles. Some of these paintings can still be seen today.

◀ *This rock art depicting a battle scene was painted on a cave wall in the Drakensberg Mountains thousands of years ago.*

▲ *South African music and dance draws from many different influences. This is a Zulu tribal dance.*

Music mixture

Two popular forms of South African music, jazz and gospel, originated with West African slaves brought over by European settlers. Young people have developed their own style of music, known as *kwaito*. This is a mixture of hip-hop, R&B, raga and house music.

Religion

About 80 per cent of South Africans are Christians, although many black South Africans combine traditional African and Christian beliefs. Other religions include Hinduism, Islam and Judaism.

FAMOUS SOUTH AFRICAN

Miriam Makeba (1932–2008)

Miriam Makeba was a singer and human rights activist. She was exiled from South Africa because she spoke out against the policy of apartheid, but she used her singing and concerts around the world to draw international attention to the campaign against apartheid in her country.

Exporting South African culture

Over the years, many people have left South Africa, either to settle or to work for a few years. They often take with them things that remind them of their home country. One example of this is *biltong* – a kind of dried meat first brought to South Africa by Dutch settlers. Now it is stocked by shops all over the world in countries where South Africans have settled, and is popular with non-South Africans, too.

▼ *These men are making biltong, a South African snack of dried meat that is now eaten all over the world.*

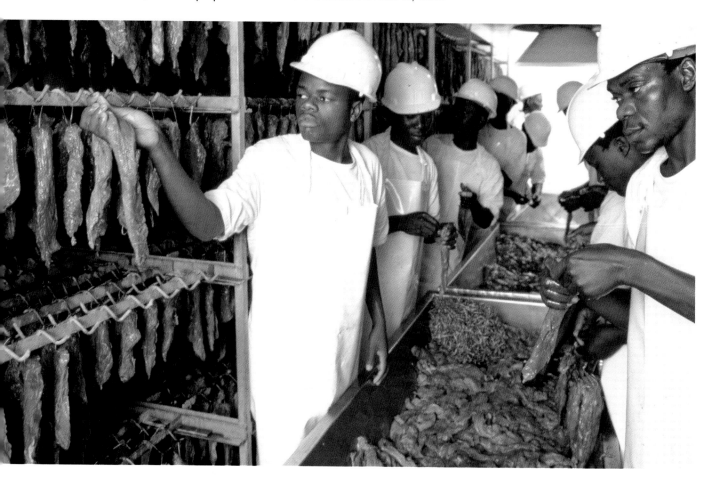

The media

Until 1975, there was no television in South Africa because the government did not want South Africans to know what was happening in other countries. Today, many of the programmes people watch are the same as those in Europe or North America, including the South African versions of *Big Brother* and *Strictly Come Dancing*. The most popular soap opera in South Africa is *Soul City*, which tackles subjects such as HIV/AIDS. It is now being broadcast in neighbouring countries such as Botswana and Zimbabwe.

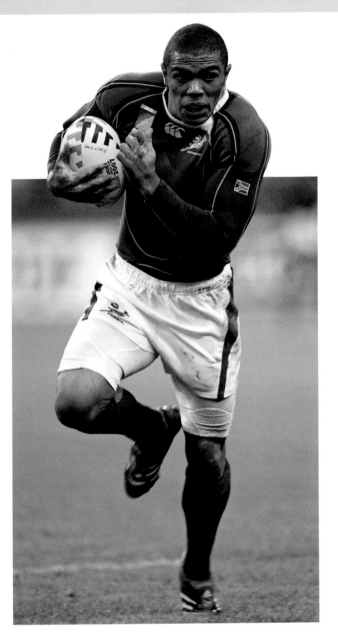

◀ *Rugby star Bryan Habana helped South Africa to its World Cup win in 2007, and was named Player of the Year by the International Rugby Board.*

★★★★★★★★★★★★★★★★★★★★★★★

FAMOUS SOUTH AFRICAN

Oscar Pistorius (b. 1986)

South African athlete Oscar Pistorius is nicknamed 'Blade Runner'. He is a double amputee who runs with the aid of carbon-fibre artificial limbs. He has been a world record holder in the Paralympics for the 100-, 200- and 400-metre events.

★★★★★★★★★★★★★★★★★★★★★★★

Sport

South Africa is a great sporting nation, and some people believe that it is through sport that all the different races of South Africa can come together. However, white and black people still tend to play different sports. White people mostly play cricket and rugby, while black people are keen football fans and players. South Africa was not allowed to take part in some sporting events during apartheid, but since then, South African teams have been successful in international events, particularly rugby. The South African rugby team won the World Cup in 1995 and 2007. In cricket, too, the national team has performed well, reaching the semi-finals of the Cricket World Cup in 2007 and the quarter-finals in 2011.

Economy and trade

Since the end of apartheid, South Africa's economy has developed rapidly, as it has been able to increase its trade with other countries. However, around 13 million people in South Africa still live on less than £1 per day.

IT'S A FACT!

South Africa has the 26th largest economy in the world. It has suffered during the economic downturn in recent years and is also hampered by electricity supply problems. However it is still Africa's biggest economy.

A growing economy

South Africa has the most important economy in Africa. It has good road and railway networks with other countries in southern Africa, as well as connections to the rest of the world. The end of apartheid meant that foreign companies started to invest in South Africa, and because of this the country's economy has grown. Until 2009, the value of all the goods and services produced in South Africa increased every year but the global economic downturn has affected economic growth.

▼ *South African grapes are exported and enjoyed all over the world. Some are made into wine.*

Natural resources

South Africa's wealth is in its natural resources. Nearly 90 per cent of all the platinum on Earth can be found in South Africa, as well as 80 per cent of the manganese, 73 per cent of the chrome and 41 per cent of the gold. There are still many more mineral deposits waiting to be exploited. South Africa is the world's third-largest producer of diamonds, and these precious stones are sent to Antwerp in Belgium and Amsterdam in the Netherlands to be cut into jewels and for other purposes.

GLOBAL LEADER

The world's largest diamond was found in South Africa in 1905. It was cut into two large diamonds and 104 smaller ones, and these now form part of the British Crown Jewels.

Trading partners

South Africa trades most with China, Germany, the USA, Saudi Arabia, Japan, Iran and the UK, and trade with other African countries is increasing. Its biggest exports are gold, diamonds, metals and minerals, machinery and equipment, as well as agricultural goods such as fruit, flowers and livestock. South Africa has the opposite seasons to Europe, so is able to supply food when it is out of season there. It imports machinery, chemicals, petroleum products and scientific equipment.

◀ *This woman is working in a factory in Durban. Manufacturing is vital to South Africa's economy, producing machinery and equipment that are sold overseas.*

Relationship with China

South Africa has benefited from the economic growth of China, and it is now China's largest trading partner in Africa. In the past decade, trade between Africa and China has trebled, and trade with South Africa made up the largest part of that. South Africa exports iron ore, copper, chrome, timber and paper pulp to China, and imports goods such as toys and electronic equipment.

GOING GLOBAL

South Africa is becoming a popular choice for international businesses to set up call centres. It has the advantages of being in more or less the same time zone as Europe, and between that of the Americas and Asia, and there are many English-speaking South Africans looking for work.

Energy

South Africa uses coal to generate most of its electricity, and the emissions from power stations make it the fourteenth highest. The country is now trying to reduce its emissions, and alternative energy sources are being considered. In the meantime, new power stations are being built to cope with demand and to prevent a serious crisis in the electricity supply.

▼ *Sasol is the world's first – and largest – oil-from-coal refinery. It provides 40 per cent of the country's fuel.*

Tourism

Tourism is one of South Africa's fastest-growing industries and is a boost to the economy. The number of foreign tourists increases every year, with a total of 7.3 million visitors in 2010, creating many job opportunities. People visit to enjoy the good weather, the beautiful scenery and the wildlife they can see in the national parks and game reserves. Some tourists are interested in South Africa's recent history and tour townships such as Soweto. Tourists come from other countries in Africa as well as North America, the UK, Russia, Hungary, Finland, India, Japan, Thailand and Singapore.

▲ *Every year, millions of tourists visit South Africa to see sights such as the penguin colonies on Boulder Beach near Cape Town.*

IT'S A FACT!

Recently, the South African government has invested in Soweto to improve the economy of this township. It has built a transport system and tourist attractions including a museum dedicated to Hector Pieterson, one of the first victims of the Soweto Uprising in the 1970s.

Government and politics

South Africa experiences many of the same economic and social problems as other African countries. However, because of its recent history, it can help promote democracy in other African nations.

Rejoining the world

One of the most important jobs for the new government in 1994 was to re-establish relationships with other countries. South Africa is now part of the African Union (AU) once more, and is an active member of the United Nations. South Africa is becoming more involved with the G8 group of countries, and has joined BRICS, the group of countries with emerging economies. The South African government has also established a partnership with the European Union.

▲ *The Union Buildings in Pretoria are the official seat of the South African government.*

IT'S A FACT!

Pretoria has the second largest number of foreign embassies in the world. Only the US capital, Washington, D.C., has more.

The parliamentary system

Each province in South Africa has its own provincial government, which is responsible for local matters such as healthcare and education. Each province sends 10 representatives to the national parliament and elections are held in South Africa every five years. In 2009 Jacob Zuma, leader of the African National Congress (ANC), became president. Earlier in his life he was imprisoned alongside Nelson Mandela on Robben Island.

GLOBAL LEADER

Dismantling nuclear weapons
In the early 1990s, South Africa became the only country in the world to voluntarily get rid of its nuclear weapons. Since then, South Africa's leaders have tried to persuade other countries to do the same.

Community projects

There are many small community projects in South Africa that help those in need. Many of these are funded by overseas aid organizations. One such project, Fancy Stitch, supports women by bringing them together to make brightly coloured handicrafts, artworks and textiles. The women create works that say something about their lives, such as HIV/AIDS, farming, livestock, cities, families, gardens, work and wildlife. They sell their products to bring in much-needed money.

▼ *Women from the Ndebele tribe sell their handicrafts to a tourist outside a craft shop at a cultural village near Johannesburg.*

Developing democracy

South Africa has demonstrated to the rest of Africa how a democracy can work. In contrast to the apartheid years, it now has a constitution that bans any form of discrimination. One party – the African National Congress (ANC) – which received 65.9 per cent of the vote in the 2009 election, dominates the government. But with a drop in support of 4 per cent from the 2004 election, the ANC will have to work hard to keep its support.

Peacekeeping

South Africa has been called on to take part in peacekeeping missions in several African countries. It has sent troops to the Democratic Republic of Congo (DRC), Sudan and Burundi. In 2008, along with many other countries, South Africa called for a ceasefire in the DRC so that aid could reach the refugees. Members of the government have also played a key role in trying to arrange peace talks between political parties, particularly in South Africa's neighbouring country Zimbabwe.

▼ *Former president Thabo Mbeki inspects South African troops sent to Sudan to help restore peace in the region in 2005.*

Problems for the government

Much has improved in South Africa, but it still faces many problems. The fact that there is still a big divide between rich and poor causes unrest, resentment and crime, which is particularly bad in the big cities. The HIV/AIDS epidemic makes this situation even worse, because money that could be used to develop the country is spent instead on caring for those with the virus.

▼ *Nelson Mandela meets children in 2005 after visiting the museum that has been opened at Robben Island, where he was imprisoned.*

FAMOUS SOUTH AFRICAN

Nelson Mandela (b. 1918)

Nelson Mandela was imprisoned in 1964 for campaigning against apartheid. He remained there for 27 years, but after his release he was elected president of South Africa. He retired in 1999 and since then he has been an ambassador for many causes, such as HIV/AIDS and poverty in Africa.

South Africa is likely to change even more rapidly between now and 2020 than it has in recent years. The changes that have been made since the end of apartheid have brought prosperity for some people, but South Africa still faces some challenges.

A modern country

Experts believe that by 2020, the number of people living in cities in South Africa could be as high as 80 per cent of the population. This means that services such as water supply and transport will need to be provided for all these people. There will be a lot of pressure on the government to provide these, as well as ensuring that there is enough housing and enough jobs for everyone.

▼ *As more people move to cities such as Durban, more housing and better public transport and health-care will be needed.*

Climate change

Climate change could have a big impact on South Africa in the next few years. Existing plants and animals would find it difficult to adapt to rising temperatures. Some species in South Africa's famous Kruger National Park are already dying out. Higher temperatures would mean there is less rain, which could reduce crop production.

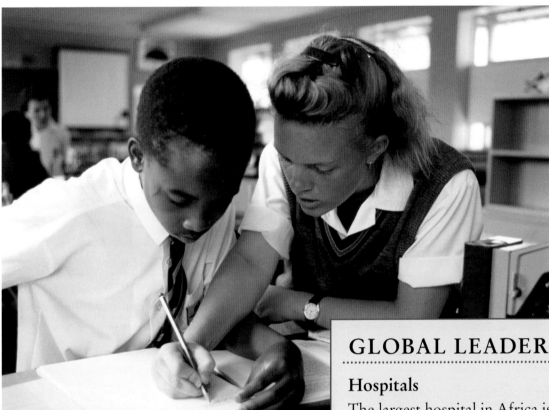

▲ *Schools in South Africa are now integrated, and accept both black and white students. It is important for black South Africans to be treated equally if the country is to develop.*

GLOBAL LEADER

Hospitals
The largest hospital in Africa is in the township of Soweto. Every day, more than 2,000 patients check into Baragwanath Hospital. Nearly half of them are HIV positive.

Development for all

The major issue of inequality must be tackled in the near future. As the economy grows, and more people move from the country to the towns and cities, the government needs to ensure that money is spent on schools, housing and hospitals so that people can be lifted out of poverty, which is at the heart of most of South Africa's problems. Unless this happens, unrest will continue.

Growing equality

Although black people and white people still tend to lead fairly separate lives, it is likely that in the future there will be more mixed schools, businesses, government and sport. South Africa's problems will be helped if the economy continues to develop and everyone benefits from the new wealth. These changes will all help South Africa become a richer and more globally important country in the future.

Glossary

African Union an international organization that promotes unity, co-operation and solidarity among African states.

ANC the African National Congress – the main political party in South Africa, based on the first liberation movement.

BRICS The group of emerging economies, named after the first initial of the countries concerned: Brazil, Russia, India, China and now South Africa.

constitution a document that lays out the main laws of a nation. Laws are not allowed to be passed that contradict a country's constitution.

continents the Earth's seven great land masses – Africa, Antarctica, Asia, Australia, Europe, North America and South America.

democracy a form of government in which people vote for the leaders they wish to represent them.

drought a water shortage caused by a long spell with little or no rain.

economy the financial system of a country or region, including how much money is made from the production and sale of goods and services.

export to transport products or materials abroad for sale or trade.

G8 a group of countries (Canada, France, Germany, Italy, Japan, Russia, the UK and the USA), that meets to discuss global economic concerns.

homelands under apartheid, areas set aside for the black African population.

immigrant a person who has moved to another country to live.

import to bring in goods or materials from a foreign country for sale.

minerals solid substances, such as limestone or quartz, that occur naturally within the earth.

national park an area of land that has been declared public property by a government in order to preserve both the land and the wildlife that lives on it.

plateau a relatively flat, high expanse of land.

refugee someone who has had to flee from their own country because of war or persecution.

resources things that are available to use, often to help develop a country's industry and economy. Resources could be minerals, workers (labour) or water.

township a settlement on the outskirts of many major South African cities, where non-white people live.

veldt a wide-open area of countryside.

wetland an area of marshy land.

Further information

Books

*Countries in the News:
South Africa*
by Michael Gallagher
(Franklin Watts, 2009)

Country File: South Africa
by Ian Graham
(Franklin Watts, 2004)

History Makers: Nelson Mandela
by Sarah Ridley
(Franklin Watts, 2009)

*South Africa: Letters from Around
the World*
by Cath Senker
(Cherrytree Books, 2009)

Welcome to South Africa
by Umaima Mulla-Feroze and
Mary-Ann Stotko
(Franklin Watts, 2006)

World Tour: South Africa
by Tonya Leslie
(Raintree, 2003)

Websites

**https://www.cia.gov/library/publications/
the-world-factbook/geos/sf.html**
Lots of facts and statistics about South Africa.

**http://www.bbc.co.uk/news/
world-africa-14094760**
The BBC's country profile, with details about South
Africa's history and people.

**http://www.nelsonmandela.org/index.php/memory/
views/biography**
A fascinating biography of South Africa's most
famous statesman.

*Every effort has been made by the publisher to ensure
that these websites contain no inappropriate or offensive
material. However, because of the nature of the Internet,
it is impossible to guarantee that the contents of these sites
will not be altered. We strongly advise that Internet access
is supervised by a responsible adult.*

Index

Numbers in **bold** indicate pictures